JAMES M. KOUZES | BA

LPI

Leadership Practices Inventory

FOURTH EDITION

WORKBOOK

UNDERSTANDING AND MAKING SENSE OF YOUR LPI FEEDBACK

Pfeiffer
A Wiley Imprint
www.pfeiffer.com

Published by Pfeiffer
An Imprint of Wiley
One Montgomery Street, Suite 1200, San Francisco, CA 94104-4594
www.pfeiffer.com

For additional copies/bulk purchases of this book in the U.S. please contact 800-274-4434.

Pfeiffer books and products are available through most bookstores. To contact Pfeiffer directly call our Customer Care Department within the U.S. at 800-274-4434, outside the U.S. at 317-572-3985, fax 317-572-4002, or visit www.pfeiffer.com.

Pfeiffer publishes in a variety of print and electronic formats and by print-on-demand. Some material included with standard print versions of this book may not be included in e-books or in print-on-demand. If this book refers to media such as a CD or DVD that is not included in the version you purchased, you may download this material at **http://booksupport.wiley.com**. For more information about Wiley products, visit **www.wiley.com**.

ISBN: 978-1-118-18273-4

Acquiring Editor: Marisa Kelley

Director of Development: Kathleen Dolan Davies

Development Editor: Janis Chan

Production Editor: Dawn Kilgore

Editor: Rebecca Taff

Manufacturing Supervisor: Becky Morgan

Designer: izles design

Printed in the United States of America

Printing   10 9 8 7 6 5 4 3 2 1

CONTENTS

Welcome

MAKE THE MOST OF YOUR LPI FEEDBACK

This probably doesn't come as any surprise to you, but there's no such thing as instant leadership—or instant expertise of any kind. Those who are the very best at anything became that way because they had a strong desire to excel, a belief that new skills and abilities can be learned, and a willing devotion to deliberate practice and continuous learning. What truly differentiates the expert performers from the good performers is hours of practice. Deliberate practice. The best leaders work at becoming the best, and it doesn't happen over a weekend.

Those who are the best at leading are also the best at learning. Exemplary leaders don't rest on their laurels or rely on their natural talents; instead, they continually do more to improve themselves. So if you want to be the best you can be, you need to become a great learner.

Here are some tips on how you can get the most learning out of the LPI process.

- *Accept the feedback as a gift.* Feedback may not come wrapped in a package with a bow, but it's still one of the most valuable gifts you'll ever receive. Why? Because we know from our research that leaders who are the most open to feedback are far more effective than leaders who resist hearing other people's perspectives on their behaviors.

- *Take the feedback seriously.* You might wonder, "Will it really make a difference if I increase the frequency of the behaviors measured by the LPI?" It will. Research consistently shows the same results: The more frequently you demonstrate the behaviors included in the LPI, the more likely you will be seen as an effective leader.

- *Value the differences in your observers' perspectives.* You're a multi-dimensional person, and your feedback ought to be multi-dimensional as well. You work with people from a variety of backgrounds and from a variety of functions and organizations. Feedback from these multiple perspectives helps you see how you lead across groups and situations. The feedback from each observer helps you build a more complete picture of how effective you are as a leader.

- *Plan now to retake the LPI.* Great leaders continually set goals and seek feedback. The LPI gives you a snapshot in time. It is a beginning point from which to move forward. To heighten your focus and practice with great purpose, decide now that you will retake the instrument within a specific period of time—we recommend between six and nine months—to see how you are doing and identify new priorities for your practice.

WHY YOU CAN TRUST THE FEEDBACK

When we developed the LPI, we conducted several tests to ensure that the instrument had sound psychometric properties. Our own, as well as independent studies, consistently confirm that the LPI has very strong reliability and validity. Reliability means that the six statements pertaining to each leadership practice are highly correlated with one another.

Test/re-test reliability is also high. This means that scores from one administration of the LPI to another within a short time span (a few days or even months) and without any significant intervening event (such as a leadership training program) are consistent and stable.

The LPI has both face validity and predictive validity. "Face validity" means that the results make sense to people. "Predictive validity" means that the results are significantly correlated with various performance measures and can be used to make predictions about leadership effectiveness.

LEADERSHIP BEHAVIORS ORGANIZED BY PRACTICE

Model the Way

1. Sets a personal example of what he/she expects of others.

6. Spends time and energy making certain that the people he/she works with adhere to the principles and standards we have agreed on.

11. Follows through on promises and commitments he/she makes.

16. Asks for feedback on how his/her actions affect other people's performance.

21. Builds consensus around a common set of values for running our organization.

26. Is clear about his/her philosophy of leadership.

Inspire a Shared Vision

2. Talks about future trends that will influence how our work gets done.

7. Describes a compelling image of what our future could be like.

12. Appeals to others to share an exciting dream of the future.

17. Shows others how their long-term interests can be realized by enlisting in a common vision.

22. Paints the "big picture" of what we aspire to accomplish.

27. Speaks with genuine conviction about the higher meaning and purpose of our work.

Challenge the Process

3. Seeks out challenging opportunities that test his/her own skills and abilities.

8. Challenges people to try out new and innovative ways to do their work.

13. Searches outside the formal boundaries of his/her organization for innovative ways to improve what we do.

18. Asks "What can we learn?" when things don't go as expected.

23. Makes certain that we set achievable goals, make concrete plans, and establish measurable milestones for the projects and programs that we work on.

28. Experiments and takes risks, even when there is a chance of failure.

Enable Others to Act

4. Develops cooperative relationships among the people he/she works with.

9. Actively listens to diverse points of view.

14. Treats others with dignity and respect.

19. Supports the decisions that people make on their own.

24. Gives people a great deal of freedom and choice in deciding how to do their work.

29. Ensures that people grow in their jobs by learning new skills and developing themselves.

Encourage the Heart

5. Praises people for a job well done.

10. Makes it a point to let people know about his/her confidence in their abilities.

15. Makes sure that people are creatively rewarded for their contributions to the success of projects.

20. Publicly recognizes people who exemplify commitment to shared values.

25. Finds ways to celebrate accomplishments.

30. Give the members of the team lots of appreciation and support for their contributions.

THE TEN COMMITMENTS OF EXEMPLARY LEADERSHIP

Model the Way

- Clarify values by finding your voice and affirming shared values.

- Set the example by aligning actions with shared values.

Inspire a Shared Vision

- Envision the future by imagining exciting and ennobling possibilities.

- Enlist others in a common vision by appealing to shared aspirations.

Challenge the Process

- Search for opportunities by seizing the initiative and by looking outward for innovative ways to improve.

- Experiment and take risks by constantly generating small wins and learning from experience.

Enable Others to Act

- Foster collaboration by building trust and facilitating relationships.

- Strengthen others by increasing self-determination and developing competence.

Encourage the Heart

- Recognize contributions by showing appreciation for individual excellence.

- Celebrate the values and victories by creating a spirit of community.

NOTES

First Impressions

To keep in mind when reviewing your LPI report:

- There is no such thing as a "bad" score, or even a "good" score. The LPI scores are a snapshot—an objective, current view of your leadership behaviors. They are not "grades" but opportunities for you to become more comfortable and skillful as a leader.

- Look for *messages* in the data, not scores. You may be receiving feedback from your manager, your direct reports, your peers, and others with whom you interact. It's easy to get lost in all the numbers. But don't let the data overwhelm you. Ask yourself, "What are people trying to tell me about my leadership behaviors?" "What am I doing or not doing that is causing people to rate me the way they do?" "Where do I see consistencies and inconsistencies?" "Where are there patterns that shape how others see my leadership?" Treat the LPI feedback not as a report card, but as valid and useful information that you can use to become a better leader.

- Take personal ownership of the scores instead of thinking up excuses for your observers' ratings. Remember that the purpose of this assessment is to identify what you can do to become a better leader.

- Remember that the observers are referred to by letters and numbers instead of by name so they remain anonymous. Do not waste your time attempting to figure out who D1 or C3 might be. It does not matter, and you are likely to be incorrect anyway. Instead, concentrate on the messages.

- Do not be surprised if one observer rates you significantly lower in most if not all of the practices. You do not interact with everyone equally; the lower rating usually indicates that that observer does not see you engaging in the practice behaviors very frequently. You might have to think about and create new ways to ensure your leadership is more visible.

Check any of the words in the list below that express what you felt when you first looked at your LPI feedback. Use the space below the list to write any other feelings you had.

☐ Amused   ☐ Pleased   ☐ Challenged

☐ Relieved   ☐ Confused   ☐ Surprised

☐ Disappointed   ☐ Upset   ☐ Angry

☐ Humbled   ☐ Anxious   ☐ Concerned

☐ Embarrassed   ☐ Neutral—
no strong feelings

☐ Other:

- -

....

1. What was your *strongest* feeling?

....
- -
....
- -
....

2. Why does this feedback make you feel that way?

....

- -

....

- -

....

3. Please describe anything in your Feedback Report that is confusing, incomplete, or contradictory.

....

- -

....

- -

....

Exploring Consistency

Consistency in behavior is important to your credibility. It lets others know that they can count on you to be consistent in your actions so they know what to expect from you.

In the ideal scenario, your Self ratings would be very consistent with your Observer ratings. But in the real world, scores are not always consistent.

There are a number of valid explanations for inconsistency in your feedback. For instance, some people know you better, people in various roles (or varying functions) have differing expectations of you, and you may behave differently with some people than with others. What's important is to understand why people rate you differently than you rate yourself and think about the extent to which you need to be consistent.

Look through your feedback report quickly, paying special attention to the Data Summary pages for each of The Five Practices. Think about the questions on the facing page. If you wish, there is space on the following page to record your thoughts.

COMPARE YOUR SELF RATINGS TO YOUR OBSERVER RATINGS

■ How consistent are your Self ratings with those of your Observers? In other words, do you rate yourself higher than, lower than, or about the same as others rate you?

■ Where are the Self and Observer ratings the most consistent?

COMPARE THE OBSERVERS' RATINGS WITH ONE ANOTHER

■ How consistent are your Observer ratings with one another? Do they tend to see your behavior in similar ways or not?

■ Where are the Observer ratings the most consistent with one another?

THINK ABOUT POSSIBLE REASONS FOR INCONSISTENCIES

■ Where are your Self ratings the most inconsistent with your Observer ratings?

■ Where are your Observer ratings most inconsistent with one another?

■ What might be some reasons for the inconsistencies?

LOOK FOR ANY "OUTLIERS"—OBSERVERS WHOSE SCORES SEEM PARTICULARLY HIGH OR PARTICULARLY LOW

■ Do any of your Observers' ratings seem extremely inconsistent with those of the others?

■ Why do you think that is so? Does it have to do with the situation? The relationship? You? Some other factors?

■ What can you learn from these outliers?

NOTES

Patterns and Messages

Any data, whether from the LPI or from another source, is only numbers or words until you can make sense of it. When you look at an impressionist painting from a few inches away, for instance, it's not much more than colored dots; it's only when you stand back that a pattern appears. In the same way, stand back from your data and see what emerges. What patterns do you see? What messages does the data give you?

LOOK AT THE LEADERSHIP BEHAVIORS RANKING PAGE

1. What three to five behaviors received the highest ratings from your observers? On your report, put a plus sign (+) next to those items. Those are the items that your observers agree you do most frequently. Copy them below.

....

....

2. What three to five behaviors received the lowest ratings from your observers? Put a minus sign (–) next to those items. Those are the items that your observers agree that you do least frequently—behaviors in which you might need the most improvement. Copy them below.

....

....

3. What do these ratings tell about where you are most comfortable and where you might need to improve?

....

- -

....

Look at the top ten behaviors on this page (the ones your observers think you engage in the most frequently) and the bottom ten behaviors (those your observers think you engage in the least frequently).

4. What patterns do you see among the ten most frequent behaviors?

....

- -

....

5. What patterns do you see among the ten least frequent behaviors?

....

- -

....

6. What do those patterns tell you?

....

- -

- -

NOTES

TURN TO THE PERCENTILE RANKING PAGE

The Percentile Ranking page of your LPI Feedback Report shows how your Self and Observer scores compare with a large sample of Observer ratings for leaders who have also taken the LPI.

Fill out the chart below by placing a check mark in the appropriate spaces for corresponding rater type, response, and percentile ranking. Then answer the questions on the next page.

PERCENTILE	MODEL THE WAY	INSPIRE A SHARED VISION	CHALLENGE THE PROCESS	ENABLE OTHERS TO ACT	ENCOURAGE THE HEART
BELOW 30TH					
Self					
Manager					
Direct Report					
Co-Worker					
Other					
30TH–70TH					
Self					
Manager					
Direct Report					
Co-Worker					
Other					
70TH–100TH					
Self					
Manager					
Direct Report					
Co-Worker					
Other					

1. Where do your scores fall in relationship to other leaders in the LPI database?

....

- -

....

- -

....

2. Does the completed chart on the previous page tell you anything new about the consistency or lack of consistency between your scores? If so, what does the chart clearly show that wasn't so noticeable on the previous pages?

....

- -

....

- -

....

3. What does this page tell you about where you are most comfortable as a leader and where you need to improve?

....

- -

....

- -

....

CONSIDER ADDITIONAL FEEDBACK

You may have received feedback on your leadership behavior from the essay section of the LPI report and from other sources, such as surveys, oral or written assessments from your manager, and interactions with others.

1. **How does the LPI feedback compare to other feedback you've received?**
Where are the messages consistent, and where are there differences?

....

- -

....

- -

2. **What might be the reasons for the differences?**

....

- -

....

- -

3. **What additional information would you like to have?** How
could you get it?

....

- -

....

- -

NOTES

Focus Your Developmental Efforts

If you want to be a leader, you have to pay attention to those leadership behaviors that seem most comfortable for you and those you don't engage in as frequently.

Take it one step at a time. Small wins create momentum for change.

According to researchers, what truly differentiates the great from the merely good or average, regardless of their fields, is hours and hours of practice in order to obtain mastery in their fields and endeavors.

It is only through deliberate practice—focused, planned learning activities designed to improve a specific aspect of performance and usually guided by a trainer or coach—that you can develop your leadership capacity. That is true whether you want to improve your strengths—the skills you already have—or strengthen your weak behaviors.

To use your LPI feedback to improve, follow these steps:

1. Use your LPI feedback to identify your priorities for improvement and set specific goals.

2. Make a plan to achieve your goals.

3. Go public with your plan.

4. Obtain feedback and support.

IDENTIFY YOUR PRIORITIES

Take another look at the Leadership Behaviors Ranking page in your LPI Feedback Report. Where would you like to focus your developmental efforts?

1. Behaviors to keep practicing

....

- -

....

2. Behaviors to strengthen

....

- -

....

Circle one behavior to maintain at current rate of frequency and one behavior to practice more frequently as your top priorities at this time. Then complete the Leadership Development Worksheet on pages 26 and 27 to set your goals for the next learning project and come up with a plan for achieving them. (There is a sample worksheet on pages 24 and 25.)

When you achieve your goals, you can choose two more priorities and repeat the process. You can download blank worksheets at **www.leadershipchallenge.com/go/lpiworksheet**.

In addition to practice, you need good coaching, and The Five Practices of Exemplary Leadership® provides a coaching framework. But remember that improvement begins by first acknowledging that you can be a better leader than you are today and that you *want to* put forth the effort to achieve that. No amount of coaching or practice can force you to improve. The motivation comes from within. But here's something we know from our research: The best leaders are the best learners.

THOSE WHO PERFORM AT THE HIGHEST LEVELS BELIEVE THAT, NO MATTER HOW GOOD THEY ARE, THEY CAN ALWAYS BE BETTER. LESS IS NOT MORE WHEN IT COMES TO LEARNING. MORE IS MORE.

NOTES

Leadership Development Worksheet

TODAY'S DATE: May 1, 2013

LEADERSHIP DEVELOPMENT PERIOD: May 2 – 22, 2013

MY TWO TOP PRIORITIES FOR THIS PERIOD: Write a compelling vision statement and present it to my team

- A LEADERSHIP BEHAVIOR TO KEEP PRACTICING: Model the Way: Continue asking for feedback from team members on how my actions affect their performance

- A LEADERSHIP BEHAVIOR TO STRENGTHEN: Inspire a Shared vision: Describe a compelling image of the future and enlist team members in that common vision

MY GOALS (WHAT I WANT TO ACHIEVE): Write and present a compelling vision of the future that my team shares

THE BENEFITS OF ACHIEVING THESE GOALS: We will be energized and enthusiastic about working together toward our common goal; we will be more productive; we will be better able to achieve our team's mission.

MY MEASURE OF SUCCESS (HOW I WILL KNOW WHEN I HAVE REACHED MY GOALS):

Team members give me feedback that lets me know they understand and share my vision

ACTIONS I WILL TAKE TO ACHIEVE MY GOALS

- ACTION: Write a 5 to 7 minute vision statement

- DATE BY WHICH I WILL TAKE THIS ACTION: May 8

- ACTION: Ask for feedback on my draft vision statement from Luis, who does this better than anyone I know, revise it, ask him to review the revised draft, and make any additional changes that might be needed

- DATE BY WHICH I WILL TAKE THIS ACTION: May 15

- ACTION: Present my vision statement to my team, ask for their feedback, revise it again, and present the revised statement to the team

- DATE BY WHICH I WILL TAKE THIS ACTION: May 22

PEOPLE WHO WILL GIVE ME FEEDBACK: Luis and my team members

PEOPLE WHO WILL PROVIDE SUPPORT: My manager, Teri, and my team members

Leadership Development Worksheet

TODAY'S DATE:

LEADERSHIP DEVELOPMENT PERIOD:

MY TWO TOP PRIORITIES FOR THIS PERIOD:

■ A LEADERSHIP BEHAVIOR TO KEEP PRACTICING:

■ A LEADERSHIP BEHAVIOR TO STRENGTHEN:

MY GOALS (WHAT I WANT TO ACHIEVE):

THE BENEFITS OF ACHIEVING THESE GOALS:

MY MEASURE OF SUCCESS (HOW I WILL KNOW WHEN I HAVE REACHED MY GOALS):

ACTIONS I WILL TAKE TO ACHIEVE MY GOALS

◼ ACTION:

◼ DATE BY WHICH I WILL TAKE THIS ACTION:

◼ ACTION:

◼ DATE BY WHICH I WILL TAKE THIS ACTION:

◼ ACTION:

◼ DATE BY WHICH I WILL TAKE THIS ACTION:

PEOPLE WHO WILL GIVE ME FEEDBACK:

PEOPLE WHO WILL PROVIDE SUPPORT:

NOTES

Go Public with Your Plan

Research has shown that people are more likely to honor their commitments when they share them with others.

1. Share your Leadership Development Plan with a colleague.
Summarize the following:

- The two top priorities that emerged from your LPI feedback and your reasons for choosing them

  ....

  -

  ....

- Your goals, the benefits of achieving those goals, the actions you will take for achieving goals, and your timetable

  ....

  -

  ....

  -

- The people who will provide feedback and support as you work toward your goals

  ....

  -

  ....

  -

2. In talking over your Leadership Development Plan with a colleague, summarize his or her feedback.

....

- -

....

- -

....

- -

3. What changes, if any, will you make to your plan, based on your colleague's feedback?

....

- -

....

- -

....

- -

Discussing Your Feedback with Your Observers

When people offer feedback, they'd like to know that you value this gift and that you intend to do something with it. Plan a conversation (or conversations) with your observers in which to do the following:

- Thank your observers for their feedback.

- Acknowledge what messages you heard and ask for any necessary clarification.

- Tell observers what you are going to do and the benefits you expect.

- Ask for their continuing feedback and support.

It's up to you whether to meet with observers as a group or one-on-one. Here are some suggestions for holding productive conversations:

- Think ahead of time about what you want to say and what you would like from the observers.

- Be honest about the feedback you received and how you felt about it. By expressing your feelings, you will more easily establish trust.

- Whether you share the actual scores or just highlight the highs, lows, and need more clarity areas is up to you. But be sure to protect your observers' anonymity by not asking them to disclose the scores they gave you.

- Listen carefully and with an open mind to what your observers have to say.

- Remember to let your observers know that you welcome their feedback and appreciate their support.

NOTES

Available Resources

We hope you have found your experience with the *Leadership Practices Inventory* (LPI) assessment insightful and worthwhile. If you are looking for everyday opportunities to make a small difference in your world, need tools to start or a community to keep inspired, obtain feedback on how you are doing, or implement a leadership development program within your organization, we can help. Here are some of the resources you can draw on as you begin or continue your leadership journey.

BOOKS

Jim and Barry's books include *The Leadership Challenge, Credibility, Encouraging the Heart, The Truth About Leadership, A Leader's Legacy, The Student Leadership Challenge,* and *The Academic Administrator's Guide to Exemplary Leadership.*

WORKBOOKS

Jim and Barry believe that an important part of the learning process is practice, practice, practice, so they have created *The Leadership Challenge Workbook, The Encouraging the Heart Workbook, Strengthening Credibility: A Leader's Workbook, The Leadership Challenge Practice Book,* and *The Leadership Challenge Vision Book.* These interactive tools are designed to be used on that proverbial Monday morning when you are faced with a problem or situation and would like to resolve the issue using their framework.

APP

The Leadership Challenge Mobile Leader Tool, a smart phone application, is a convenient way to examine and employ The Five Practices of Exemplary Leadership® and the thirty LPI behaviors in your daily life. Features of the app include a seamless request-and-receive feedback process through which overall leadership performance can be tracked and measured, helpful action planning routines, model overview, and an inspirational quote of the day.

VIDEOS

These visual aids to The Leadership Challenge program bring inspiring, real-life examples to the leadership development process. There are multiple video case examples of each of The Five Practices of Exemplary Leadership.

WORKSHOP

The Leadership Challenge Workshop is a unique, intensive program that consistently receives rave reviews from attendees. It has served as a catalyst for profound leadership transformation in organizations of all sizes and in all industries. The program is highly interactive and stimulating. Participants experience and apply Jim and Barry's leadership model through video cases, workbook activities, group problem-solving tasks, lectures, and outdoor action learning. Quite often we hear workshop attendees describe how The Leadership Challenge is more than a training event and talk about how it changed their lives. It's a bold statement, we know, but we've watched it happen time after time, leader after leader.

Combined, these resources truly make Jim and Barry the most trusted sources for becoming a better leader. To find out more about these products, please visit **www.leadershipchallenge.com**. If you would like to speak to a leadership consultant about bringing The Leadership Challenge to your organization or team, call 866-888-5159 (toll free).

Further Reading

GENERAL LEADERSHIP

Burlingham, B. *Small Giants: Companies That Choose to Be Great Instead of Big.*
New York: Penguin Group, 2005.

Collins, J. *Good to Great: Why Some Companies Make the Leap and Others Don't.*
New York: HarperCollins, 2001.

Collins, J. *Great by Choice: Uncertainty, Chaos, and Luck: Why Some Companies Thrive
Despite Them All.* New York: HarperCollins, 2011.

Gallos, J. V. (Ed.). *Business Leadership: A Jossey-Bass Reader.* San Francisco:
Jossey-Bass, 2003.

Hamel, G. *What Matters Now: How to Win in a World of Relentless Change, Ferocious
Competition, and Unstoppable Innovation.* San Francisco: Jossey-Bass, 2012.

Hamm, J. *Unusually Excellent: The Necessary Nine Skills Required for the Practice of
Great Leadership.* San Francisco: Jossey-Bass, 2011.

Heifitz, R. A., and Linsky, M. *Leadership on the Line: Staying Alive Through the Dangers
of Leading.* Boston: Harvard Business School Press, 2002.

Kawaski, G. *Enchantment: The Art of Changing Hearts, Minds, and Actions.* New York:
Portfolio, 2011.

Kouzes, J. M., and Posner, B. Z. *The Truth About Leadership: The No-Fads,
Heart-of-the-Matter Facts You Need to Know.* San Francisco: Jossey-Bass, 2010.

Peters, T. *Re-Imagine! Business Excellence in a Disruptive Age.* New York:
DK Publishing, Inc., 2003.

Pfeffer, J. *What Were They Thinking?: Unconventional Wisdom About Management.*
Boston: Harvard Business School Press, 2007.

Porras, J., Emery, S., and Thompson, M. *Success Built to Last: Creating a Life That
Matters.* Upper Saddle River, NJ: Wharton School Publishing, 2006.

Thompson, R. H. *The Offsite: A Leadership Challenge Fable.* San Francisco:
Jossey-Bass, 2008

MODEL THE WAY

Block, P. *The Answer to How Is Yes: Acting On What Matters.* San Francisco: Berrett-Koehler, 2002.

Conant, D., and Norgaard, M. *TouchPoints: Creating Powerful Leadership Connections in the Smallest of Moments.* San Francisco: Jossey-Bass, 2011.

DePree, M. *Leadership Is an Art.* New York: Doubleday, 2004.

George, B. *True North: Discover Your Authentic Leadership.* San Francisco: Jossey-Bass, 2007.

Goleman, D. *Social Intelligence: The New Science of Human Relationships.* New York: Bantam, 2006.

Kouzes, J. M., and B. Z. Posner. *Credibility: How Leaders Gain and Lose It, Why People Demand* (2nd ed.). San Francisco: Jossey-Bass, 2011.

Kraemer, H. M. J., Jr. *From Values to Action: The Four Principles of Values-Based Leadership.* San Francisco: Jossey-Bass, 2011.

Maister, D. *Practice What You Preach: What Managers Must Do to Create a High Achievement Culture.* New York: The Free Press, 2001.

Palmer, P. *Let Your Life Speak: Listening to the Voice of Vocation.* San Francisco: Jossey-Bass, 2000.

Pearce, T. *Leading Out Loud: Inspiring Change Through Authentic Communications* (new and revised). San Francisco: Jossey-Bass, 2003.

Rhoads, A., with Shepherdson, N. *Built on Values: Creating an Enviable Culture That Outperforms the Competition.* San Francisco: Jossey-Bass, 2011.

Schein, E. *Organizational Culture and Leadership* (4th ed.). San Francisco: Jossey-Bass, 2010.

INSPIRE A SHARED VISION

Burns, J. M. *Transforming Leadership.* New York: Atlantic Books, 2003.

Clarke, B., and Crossland, R. *The Leader's Voice: How Your Communication Can Inspire Action and Get Results!* New York: SelectBooks, 2002.

Fredrickson, B. L. *Positivity: Groundbreaking Research Reveals How to Embrace the Hidden Strengths of Positive Emotions, Overcome Negativity, and Thrive.* New York: Crown, 2009.

Geary, J. *I Is an Other: The Secret Life of Metaphor and How It Shapes the Way We See the World.* New York: Harper, 2011.

Heath, C., and Heath, D. *Made to Stick: Why Some Ideas Survive and Others Die.* New York: Random House, 2007.

Leider, J., and Shapiro, D. *Whistle While You Work: Heeding Your Life's Calling.* San Francisco: Berrett-Koehler, 2001.

Maxwell, J. C. *Developing the Leader Within You* (rev. ed.). New York: Nelson Books, 2005.

Naisbitt, J. *Mindset: Reset Your Thinking and See the Future.* New York: HarperCollins, 2006.

Pink, D. *Drive: The Surprising Truth About What Motivates Us.* New York: Penguin Group, 2009.

Schuster, J. P. *The Power of Your Past: The Art of Recalling, Recasting, and Reclaiming.* San Francisco: Berrett-Koehler, 2011.

Sinek, S. *Start with Why: How Great Leaders Inspire Everyone to Take Action.* New York: Portfolio, 2010.

Spence, R. M. *It's Not What You Sell, It's What You Stand For: Why Every Extraordinary Business Is Driven by Purpose.* New York: Portfolio, 2010.

Sullenberger, C. B. *Making a Difference: Stories of Vision and Courage from America's Leaders.* New York: William Morrow, 2012.

Ulrich, D., and Ulrich, W. *The Why of Work: How Great Leaders Build Abundant Organizations That Win.* New York: McGraw-Hill, 2010.

Wheatley, M. *Turning to One Another: Simple Conversations to Restore Hope to the Future (2nd.* ed.). San Francisco: Berrett-Koehler, 2009.

CHALLENGE THE PROCESS

Amabile, T. A., and Kramer, S. J. *The Progress Principle: Using Small Wins to Ignite Joy, Engagement, and Creativity at Work.* Boston: Harvard Business Review Press, 2011.

Ariely, D. *Predictably Irrational: The Hidden Forces That Shape Our Decisions* (rev. and expanded). New York: HarperCollins, 2009.

Blum, A. *Annapurna: A Woman's Place* (20th ann. ed.). San Francisco: Sierra Club Books, 1998.

Csikszentmihalyi, M. *Flow: The Psychology of Optimal Experience.* New York: Harper, 2008.

Davila, T., Epstein, M. J., and Shelton, R. *Making Innovation Work: How to Manage It, Measure It, and Profit from It.* Upper Saddle River, NJ: Wharton School Publishing, 2006.

Farson, R., and Keyes, R. *Whoever Makes the Most Mistakes Wins: The Paradox of Innovation.* New York: The Free Press, 2002.

Foster, R., and Kaplan, S. *Creative Destruction: Why Companies That Are Built to Last Underperform the Market—and How to Successfully Transform Them.* New York: Currency, 2001.

Gladwell, M. *Blink: The Power of Thinking Without Thinking.* New York: Little, Brown and Company, 2005.

Johnson, S. *Where Good Ideas Come From: The Natural History of Innovation.* New York: Riverhead, 2010.

Kelley, T., with Littman, J. *The Art of Innovation: Lessons in Creativity from IDEO, America's Leading Design Firm.* New York: Currency Doubleday, 2001.

Klein, G. *Intuition at Work: Why Developing Your Gut Instincts Will Make You Better at What You Do.* New York: Currency Doubleday, 2002.

Seligman, M.E.P. *Flourish: A Visionary New Understanding of Happiness and Well-Being.* New York: The Free Press, 2011.

Sims, P. *Little Bets: How Breakthrough Ideas Emerge from Small Discoveries.* New York: The Free Press, 2011.

Yamashita, K., and Spataro, S. *Unstuck: A Tool for Yourself, Your Team, and Your World* (rev. ed.). New York: Portfolio/Penguin Group, 2007.

Zander, R. S., and Zander, B. *The Art of Possibility: Transforming Professional and Personal Life.* New York: Penguin Group, 2002.

ENABLE OTHERS TO ACT

Boyatzis, R., and McKee, A. *Resonant Leadership.* Boston: Harvard Business School Press, 2004.

Brooks, D. *The Social Animal: Hidden Sources of Love, Character, and Achievement.* New York: Random House, 2011.

Burchell, M., and Robin, J. *The Great Workplace: How to Build It, How to Keep It, and Why It Matters.* San Francisco: Jossey-Bass, 2011.

Cherniss, C., and Goleman, D. (Eds.). *The Emotionally Intelligent Workplace: How to Select for, Measure, and Improve Emotional Intelligence in Individuals, Groups, and Organizations.* San Francisco: Jossey-Bass, 2001.

Covey, S. M., Merrill, R. R., and Covey, S. R. *The SPEED of Trust: The One Thing That Changes Everything.* New York: The Free Press, 2006.

Farber, S. *Greater Than Yourself: The Ultimate Lesson of True Leadership.* New York: Doubleday, 2009.

Gladwell, M. *The Tipping Point: How Little Things Make a Big Difference.* Boston: Little, Brown and Company, 2000.

Hansen, M. T. *Collaboration: How Leaders Avoid the Traps, Create Unity, and Reap Big Results.* Boston: Harvard Business School Press, 2009.

Hughes, M. M., Patterson, L. B., and Terrell, J. B. *Emotional Intelligence in Action: Training and Coaching Activities for Leaders and Managers.* San Francisco: Pfeiffer, 2005.

Hurley, R. F. *The Decision to Trust: How Leaders Create High-Trust Organizations.* San Francisco: Jossey-Bass, 2012.

Kanter, R. M. *Confidence: How Winning Streaks and Losing Streaks Begin and End.* New York: Crown Business, 2004.

Lencioni, P. M. *The Five Dysfunctions of a Team: A Leadership Fable.* San Francisco: Jossey-Bass, 2002.

Maddi, S. R., and Khoshaba, D. M. *Resilience at Work: How to Succeed No Matter What Life Throws at You.* New York: American Management Association, 2005.

Merchant, N. *The New How: Creating Business Solutions Through Collaborative Strategy.* San Francisco: O'Reilly Media, 2010.

O'Reilly, C., and Pfeffer, J. *Hidden Value: How Great Companies Achieve Extraordinary Results with Ordinary People.* Boston: Harvard Business School Press, 2000.

Shockley-Zalabak, P. S., Morreale, S. and Hackman, M. *Building the High-Trust Organization: Strategies for Supporting Five Key Dimensions of Trust.* San Francisco: Jossey-Bass, 2010.

Wiseman, L. *Multipliers: How the Best Leaders Make Everyone Smarter.* New York: HarperCollins, 2010.

ENCOURAGE THE HEART

Achor, S. *The Happiness Advantage: The Seven Principles of Positive Psychology That Fuel Success and Performance at Work.* New York: Crown Books, 2010.

Blanchard, K., and Bowles, S. *High Five! The Magic of Working Together.* New York: William Morrow, 2000.

Blanchard, K., Lacinak, T., Tompkins, C., and Ballard, J. *Whale Done! The Power of Positive Relationships.* New York: The Free Press, 2002.

Cameron, K. S., Dutton, J. E., and Quinn, R. E. (Eds.). *Positive Organizational Scholarship: Foundations of a New Discipline.* San Francisco: Berrett-Koehler, 2003.

Deal, T. E., and Key, M. K. Corporate Celebrations: *Play, Purpose, and Profit at Work.* San Francisco: Berrett-Koehler, 1998.

Goffee, R., and Jones, G. *Why Should Anyone Be Led by YOU?* Boston: Harvard Business School Press, 2006.

Gostick, A., and Elton, C. *All In: How the Best Managers Create a Culture of Belief and Drive Big Results.* New York: The Free Press, 2012

Kaye, B., and Jordan-Evans, S. *Love 'Em or Lose 'Em: Getting Good People to Stay* (4th ed.). San Francisco: Berrett-Koehler, 2008.

Kouzes, J. M., and Posner, B. Z. *Encouraging the Heart: A Leader's Guide to Rewarding and Recognizing Others.* San Francisco: Jossey-Bass, 2003.

Rath, T., and Clifton, D. O. *How Full Is Your Bucket? Positive Strategies for Work and Life.* New York: Gallup Press, 2004.

Rath, T., and Harter, J. *Well-Being: The Five Essential Elements.* New York: Gallup Press, 2010.

Seligman, M. E. *Flourish: A Visionary New Understanding of Happiness and Well-Being.* New York: The Free Press, 2011.

Ventrice, C. *Make Their Day! Employee Recognition That Works.* San Francisco: Berrett-Koehler, 2003.

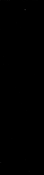

Jim Kouzes and Barry Posner

Jim Kouzes and Barry Posner have been working together for more than thirty years, studying leaders, researching leadership, conducting leadership development seminars, and serving as leaders themselves in various capacities. They are coauthors of the award-winning, best-selling book *The Leadership Challenge*. Since its first edition in 1987, *The Leadership Challenge* has sold more than two million copies worldwide and is available in more than twenty-two languages. It has won numerous awards, including the Critics' Choice Award from the nation's book review editors and the James A. Hamilton Hospital Administrators' Book of the Year Award, and was selected as one of the top ten books on leadership in Covert and Sattersten's *Top 100 Business Books of All Time*.

Jim and Barry have coauthored more than a dozen other award-winning leadership books, including *Credibility: How Leaders Gain and Lose It, Why People Demand It; The Truth about Leadership: The No-Fads, Heart-of-the-Matter Facts You Need to Know; A Leader's Legacy; Encouraging the Heart; The Student Leadership Challenge;* and *The Academic Administrator's Guide to Exemplary Leadership*. They also developed the highly acclaimed Leadership Practices Inventory (LPI), a 360-degree questionnaire for assessing leadership behavior, which is one of the most widely used leadership assessment instruments in the world, along with The Student LPI. The Five Practices of Exemplary Leadership® model which they developed has been the basis of more than five hundred doctoral dissertations and academic research projects (a summary of these are available on the web at **www.theleadershipchallenge.com/research**).

Among the honors and awards that Jim and Barry have received is the American Society for Training and Development's highest award for their Distinguished Contribution to Workplace Learning and Performance. They have been named Management/Leadership Educators of the Year by the International Management

Council; ranked by *Leadership Excellence* magazine in the top twenty on its list of the Top 100 Thought Leaders; named among the Top 50 Leadership Coaches in the nation (according to *Coaching for Leadership*); and listed among *HR Magazine*'s Most Influential International Thinkers.

Jim and Barry are frequent speakers, and each has conducted leadership development programs for organizations such as Apple, Applied Materials, ARCO, AT&T, Australia Institute of Management, Australia Post, Bank of America, Bose, Charles Schwab, Cisco Systems, Clorox, Community Leadership Association, Conference Board of Canada, Consumers Energy, Deloitte Touche, Dorothy Wylie Nursing Leadership Institute, Dow Chemical, Egon Zehnder International, Federal Express, Genentech, Google, Gymboree, HP, IBM, Jobs DR-Singapore, Johnson & Johnson, Kaiser Foundation Health Plans and Hospitals, Intel, Itau Unibanco, L. L. Bean, Lawrence Livermore National Labs, Lucile Packard Children's Hospital, Merck, Motorola, NetApp, Northrop Grumman, Novartis, Nvidia, Oakwood Housing, Oracle, Petronas, Roche Bioscience, Siemens, 3M, Toyota, United Way, USAA, Verizon, VISA, the Walt Disney Company, and Westpac. They have lectured at over sixty college and university campuses

JIM KOUZES

Kouzes is the Dean's Executive Fellow of Leadership, Leavey School of Business, at Santa Clara University, and lectures on leadership around the world to corporations, governments, and nonprofits. He is a highly regarded leadership scholar and an experienced executive; the *Wall Street Journal* cited him as one of the twelve best executive educators in the United States. In 2010, Jim received the Thought Leadership Award from the Instructional Systems Association, the most prestigious award given by the trade association of training and development industry providers. In 2006, Jim was presented with the Golden Gavel, the highest honor awarded by Toastmasters International. Jim served as president, CEO, and chairman of the Tom Peters Company from 1988 through 1999, and prior to that led the Executive Development Center at Santa Clara University (1981-1987). Jim founded the Joint Center for Human Services Development at San Jose State University (1972-1980) and was on the staff of the School of Social Work, University of Texas. His career in training and development began in 1969 when he conducted seminars for Community

Action Agency staff and volunteers in the war on poverty. Following graduation from Michigan State University (BA degree with honors in political science), he served as a Peace Corps volunteer (1967-1969). Jim can be reached at **jim@kouzes.com**.

BARRY POSNER is Accolti Professor of Leadership at the Leavey School of Business, Santa Clara University, where he served as dean of the school for twelve years (1997-2009). He has been a distinguished visiting professor at Hong Kong University of Science and Technology, Sabanci University (Istanbul), and the University of Western Australia. At Santa Clara he has received the President's Distinguished Faculty Award, the School's Extraordinary Faculty Award, and several other teaching and academic honors. An internationally renowned scholar and educator, Barry is author or coauthor of more than a hundred research and practitioner-focused articles. He currently serves on the editorial advisory boards for *Leadership and Organizational Development* and *The International Journal of Servant-Leadership*. In 2011, he received the Outstanding Scholar Award from the *Journal of Management Inquiry*.

Barry received his BA (with honors) in political science from the University of California, Santa Barbara; his MA in public administration from The Ohio State University; and his Ph.D. in organizational behavior and administrative theory from the University of Massachusetts, Amherst. Having consulted with a wide variety of public and private sector organizations around the globe, Barry also works at a strategic level with a number of community-based and professional organizations, currently sitting on the board of directors of EMQ FamiliesFirst and the Global Women's Leadership Network. He has served previously on the boards of the American Institute of Architects (AIA), Big Brothers/Big Sisters of Santa Clara County, Center for Excellence in Nonprofits, Junior Achievement of Silicon Valley and Monterey Bay, Public Allies, San Jose Repertory Theater, Sigma Phi Epsilon Fraternity, and several start-up companies. Barry can be reached at **bposner@scu.edu**.

More information about Jim and Barry and their work, research, and services can be found at **www.theleadershipchallenge.com**.

NOTES